What You Can Do With Your Will Power

By
Russell H. Conwell

What You Can Do With Your Will Power

I

Success has no secret. Her voice is forever ringing through the marketplace and crying in the wilderness, and the burden of her cry is one word — WILL. Any normal young man who hears and heeds that cry is equipped fully to climb to the very heights of life.

The message I would like to leave with the young men and women of America is a message I have been trying humbly to deliver from lecture platform and pulpit for more than fifty years. It is a message the accuracy of which has been affirmed and reaffirmed in thousands of lives whose progress I have been privileged to watch. And the message is this: Your future stands before you like a block of unwrought marble. You can work it into what you will. Neither heredity, nor environment, nor any obstacles superimposed by man can keep you from marching straight through to success, provided you are guided by a firm, driving determination and have normal health and intelligence.

Determination is the battery that commands every road of life. It is the armor against which the missiles of adversity rattle harmlessly. If there is one thing I have tried peculiarly to do through these years it is to indent in the minds of the youth of America the living fact that when they give WILL the reins and say "DRIVE" they are headed toward the heights.

The institution out of which Temple University, of Philadelphia, grew was founded thirty years ago expressly to furnish opportunities for higher education to poor boys and girls who are willing to work for it. I have seen ninety thousand students enter its doors. A very large percentage of these came to Philadelphia without money, but firmly determined to get an education. I have never known one of them to go back defeated. Determination has the properties of a powerful acid; all shackles melt before it.

Conversely, lack of will power is the readiest weapon in the arsenal of failure. The most hopeless proposition in the world is the fellow who thinks that success is a door through which he will sometime stumble if he roams around long enough. Some men seem to expect ravens to feed them, the cruse of oil to remain inexhaustible, the fish to come right up over the side of the boat at meal-time. They believethat life is a series of miracles. They loaf about and trust in their lucky star, and boldly declare that the world owes them a living.

As a matter of fact the world owes a man nothing that he does not earn. In this life a man gets about what he is worth, and he must render an equivalent for what is given him. There is no such thing as inactive success.

My mind is running back over the stories of thousands of boys and girls I have known and known about, who have faced every sort of a handicap and have won out solely by will and perseverance in working with all the power that God had given them. It is now nearly thirty years since a young English boy came into my office. He wanted to attend the evening classes at our university to learn oratory.

"Why don't you go into the law?" I asked him.

"I'm too poor! I haven't a chance!" he replied, shaking his head sadly.

I turned on him sharply. "Of course you haven't a chance," I exclaimed, "if you don't make up your mind to it!"

The next night he knocked at my door again. His face was radiant and there was a light of determination in his eyes.

"I have decided to become a lawyer," he said, and I knew from the ring of his voice that he meant it.

Many times after he became mayor of Philadelphia he must have looked back on that decision as the turning-point in his life.

I am thinking of a young Connecticut farm lad who was given up by his teachers as too weak-minded to learn. He left school when he was seven years old and toiled on his father's farm until he was twenty-one. Then something turned his mind toward the origin and development of the animal kingdom. He began to read works on zoology, and, in order to enlarge his capacity for understanding, went back to school and picked up where he left off fourteen years before. Somebody said to him, "You can get to the top if you will!"

He grasped the hope and nurtured it, until at last it completely possessed him. He entered college at twenty-eight and worked his way through with the assistance that we were able to furnish him. To-day he is a respected professor of zoology in an Ohio college.

Such illustrations I could multiply indefinitely. Of all the boys whom I have tried to help through college I cannot think of a single one who has failed for any other reason than ill health. But of course I have never helped any one who was not first helping himself. As soon as a man determines the goal toward which he is marching, he is in a strategic position to see and seize everything that will contribute toward that end.

Whenever a young man tells me that if he "had his way" he would be a lawyer, or an engineer, or what not, I always reply:

"You can be what you will, provided that it is something the world will be demanding ten years hence."

This brings to my mind a certain stipulation which the ambition of youth must recognize. You must invest yourself or your money in aknown demand. You must select an occupation that is fitted to your own special genius and to some actual want of the people. Choose as early as possible what your life-work will be. Then you can be continually equipping yourself by reading and observing to a purpose. There are many things which the average boy or girl learns in school that could be learned outside just as well.

Almost any man should be able to become wealthy in this land of opulent opportunity. There are some people who think that to be pious they must be very poor and very dirty. They are wrong. Not money, but the love of money, is the root of all evil. Money in itself is a dynamic force for helping humanity.

In my lectures I have borne heavily on the fact that we are all walking over acres of diamonds and mines of gold. There are people who think that their fortune lies in some far country. It is much more likely to lie right in their own back yards or on their front door-step, hidden from their unseeing eye. Most of our millionaires discovered their fortunes by simply looking around them.

Recently I have been investigating the lives of four thousand and forty-three American millionaires. All but twenty of them started life as poor boys, and all but forty of them have contributed largely to their communities, and divided fairly with their employees as they went along. But, alas, not one rich man's son out of seventeen dies rich.

But if a man has dilly-dallied through a certain space of wasted years, can he then develop the character—the motor force—to drive him to success? Why, my friend, will power cannot only be developed, but it is often dry powder which needs only a match. Very frequently I think of the life of Abraham Lincoln—that wonderful man! and I am thankful that I was permitted to meet him. Yet Abraham Lincoln developed the splendid sinews of his will after he was twenty-one. Before that he was just a roving, good-natured sort of a chap. Always have I regretted that I failed to ask him what special circumstance broke the chrysalis of his life and loosened the wings of his will.

Many years ago some of the students of Temple University held a meeting in a building opposite the Bellevue-Stratford Hotel. As they were leaving the building they noticed a foreigner selling peanuts on the opposite curb. While buying peanuts they got to talking with the fellow, and told him that any one could obtain an education if he was willing to work for it. Eagerly the poor fellow drank up all the information he could get. He enrolled at Temple University and worked his way through, starting with the elementary studies. He is to-day an eminent practising physician in the national capital.

Often I think of an office clerk who reached a decision that the ambitions which were stirring in his soul could be realized if he could only get an education. He attended our evening classes and was graduated with a B.S. degree. He is now the millionaire head of one of the largest brokerage houses in the country.

"Where there's a will there's a way!" But one needs to use a little common sense about selecting the way. A general may determine to win a victory, but if he hurls his troops across an open field straight into the leaden sweep of the enemy's artillery he invites disaster and defeat. The best general lays his plans carefully, and advances his troops in the way that will best conserve their strength and numbers. So must a man plan his campaign of life.

No man has a right, either for himself or for others, to be at work in a factory, or a store, or anywhere else, unless he would work there from choice — money or no money — if he had the necessities of life.

"As a man thinks, so he is," says the writer of Proverbs; but as a man adjusts himself, so really is he, after all. One great trouble with many individuals is that they are made up of all sorts of machinery that is not adjusted, that is out of place — no belts on the wheels, no fire under the boiler, hence no steam to move the mechanism.

Some folk never take the trouble to size themselves up — to find out what they are fitted to do — and then wonder why they remain way down at the bottom of the heap. I remember a young woman who told me that she did not believe she could ever be of any particular use in the world. I mentioned a dozen things that she ought to be able to do.

"If you only knew yourself," I said, "you would set yourself to writing. You ought to be an author."

She shook her head and smiled, as if she thought I was making fun of her. Later, force of circumstances drove her to take up the pen. And when she came to me and told me that she was making three thousand dollars a year in literary work, and was soon to go higher, I thought back to the time when she was a poor girl making three dollars a week when she failed accurately to estimate herself.

There is a

deplorable tendency —

II

There is a deplorable tendency among many people to wait for a particularly favorable opportunity to declare themselves in the battle of life. Some people pause for the rap of opportunity when opportunity has been playing a tattoo on their resonant skulls for years.

Hardly a single great invention has been placed on the market without a number of men putting forth the claim that they had the idea first—and in most cases they proved the fact. But while they were sitting down and dreaming, or trying to bring the device to a greater perfection, a man with initiative rose up and acted. The telegraph, telephone, sewing-machine, air-brake, mowing-machine, wireless, and linotype-machine are only a few illustrations.

The most wonderful idea is quite valueless until it is put into practical operation. The Government rewards the man who first gets a patent or first puts his invention into practical use—and the world does likewise. Thus the dreamer must always lag behind the door.

True will power also predicates concentration. I shall never forget the time I went to see President Lincoln to ask him to spare the life of one of my soldiers who was sentenced to be shot. As I walked toward the door of his office I felt a greater fear than I had ever known when the shells were bursting all about us at Antietam. Finally I mustered up courage to knock on the door. I heard a voice inside yell:

"Come in and sit down!"

The man at the table did not look up as I entered; he was busy over a bunch of papers. I sat down at the edge of a chair and wished I were in Peking or Patagonia. He never looked up until he had quite finished with the papers. Then he turned to me and said:

"I am a very busy man and have only a few minutes to spare. Tell me in the fewest words what it is you want."

As soon as I mentioned the case he said:

"I have heard all about it, and you do not need to tell me any more. Mr. Stanton was talking to me about that only a few days ago. You can go to the hotel and rest assured that the President never did sign an order to shoot a boy under twenty, and never will. You may tell his mother that." Then, after a short conversation, he took hold of another bunch of papers and said, decidedly, "Good morning!"

Lincoln, one of the greatest men of the world, owed his success largely to one rule: whatsoever he had to do at all he put his whole mind into, and held it all there until the task was all done. That makes men great almost anywhere.

Too many people are satisfied if they have done a thing "well enough." That is a fatal complacency. "Well enough" has cursed souls. "Well enough" has wrecked enterprises. "Well enough" has destroyed nations. If perfection in a task can possibly be reached, nothing short of perfection is "well enough." Governor Talbot of Massachusetts got his high office because General Swift made a happy application of the truth in saying to the convention, "I nominate for Governor of this state a man who, when he was a farmer's boy, hoed to the end of the row." That saying became a campaign slogan all up and down the state. "He hoed to the end of the row! He hoed to the end of the row!" When the people discovered that this was one of the characteristics of the man, they elected him by one of the greatest majorities ever given a Governor in Massachusetts.

Yet we must bear in mind that there is such a thing as overdoing anything. Young people should draw a line between study that secures wisdom and study that breaks down the mind; between exercise that is healthful and exercise that is injurious; between a conscientiousness that is pure and divine and a conscientiousness that is over-morbid and insane; between economy that is careful and economy that is stingy; between industry that is a reasonable use of their powers and industry that is an over-use of their powers, leading only to destruction.

The best ordered mind is one that can grasp the problems that gather around a man constantly and work them out to a logical conclusion; that sees quickly what anything means, whether it be an exhibition of goods, a juxtaposition of events, or the suggestions of literature.

A man is made up largely of his daily observations. School training serves to fit and discipline him so that he may read rightly the lesson of the things he sees around him. Men have made mighty fortunes by just using their eyes.

Several years ago I took dinner in New York with one of the great millionaires of that city. In the course of our talk he told me something about his boyhood days—how, with hardly a penny in his pocket, he slung a pack on his back and set out along the Erie Canal, looking for a job. At last he got one. He was paid three dollars a week to make soft soap for the laborers to use at the locks in washing their hands. One can hardly imagine a more humble occupation; but this boy kept his eyes open. He saw the disadvantages of soft soap, and set to work to make a hard substitute for it. Finally he succeeded, and his success brought him many, many millions.

Every person is designed for a definite work in life, fitted for a particular sphere. Before God he has a right to that sphere. If you are an excellent housekeeper you should not be running a loom, and it is your duty to prepare yourself to enter at the first opportunity the sphere for which you are fitted.

George W. Childs, who owned the Philadelphia Ledger, once blacked boots and sold newspapers in front of the Ledger building. He told me how he used to look at that building and declare over and over to himself that some day he would own the great newspaper establishment that it housed. When he mentioned his ambition to his associates they laughed at him. But Childs had indomitable grit, and ultimately he did come to own that newspaper establishment, one of the finest in the country.

Another thing very necessary to the pursuit of success is the proper employment of waiting moments. How do you use your waiting time for meals, for trains, for business? I suppose that if the average individual were to employ wisely these intervals in which he whistles and twiddles his thumbs he would soon accumulate enough knowledge to quite make over his life.

I went through the United States Senate in 1867 and asked each of the members how he got his early education. I found that an extremely large percentage of them had simply properly applied their waiting moments. Even Charles Sumner, a university graduate, told me that he learned more from the books he read outside of college than from those he had studied within. General Burnside, who was then a Senator, said that he had always had a book beside him in the shop where he worked.

Before leaving the subject of the power of the will, there is one thing I would like to say: a true will must have a decent regard for the happiness of others. Do not get so wrapped up in your own mission that you forget to be kind to other people, for you have not fulfilled every duty unless you have fulfilled the duty of being pleasant. Enemies and ignorance are the two most expensive things in a man's life. I never make unnecessary enemies—they cost too much.

Every one has within himself the tools necessary to carve out success. Consecrate yourself to some definite mission in life, and let it be a mission that will benefit the world as well as yourself. Remember that nothing can withstand the sweep of a determined will—unless it happens to be another will equally as determined. Keep clean, fight hard, pick your openings judiciously, and have your eyes forever fixed on the heights toward which you are headed. If there be any other formula for success, I do not know it.

The biography of

that great patriot—

III

The biography of that great patriot and statesman, Daniel Manin of Venice, Italy, contains a very romantic example of the possibilities of will force. He was born in a poor quarter of the city; his parents were without rank or money. Venice in 1805 was under the Austrian rule and was sharply divided into aristocratic and peasant classes. He was soon deserted by his father and left to the support of his mother. He was a dull boy, and could not keep along with other boys in the church schools; his mind labored as slowly as did the childhood intellects of many of the greatest men of history. Daniel seemed destined to earn his living digging mud out of the canals, if he supported himself at all. No American boy can be handicapped like that. But the children who learn slowly learn surely, and history, which is but the biography of great men, mentions again and again the fact that the great characters began to be able to acquire learning late in life. Napoleon and Wellington were both dull boys, and Lincoln often said that he was a dunce through his early years. Daniel Manin seems to have been utterly unable to learn from books until he was eight or ten years old. But his latent will power was suddenly developed to an unexpected degree when he was quite a youth. Kossuth, who was a personal friend of Manin, said in an address in New York that the American Republic was responsible for the awakening of Manin, and through him had made Italy free.

It appears that an American sea-captain, while discharging a cargo in Venice, employed Daniel as an errand-boy, and when the ship sailed the captain made Daniel a present of a gilt-edged copy of the lives of George Washington and John Hancock in one volume. The captain, who had greatly endeared himself to Daniel, made the boy promise solemnly that he would learn to read the book. But Daniel was utterly ignorant of the English language in print and had learned only a few phrases from the captain. The gift of that book made Venice a republic, led to the adoption of sections of the United States Constitution by that state and carried the principles on into the constitution of United Italy. That book awakened the sleeping will power of the industrious dull boy. Even his mother protested against his waste of time in trying to read English when he was unable to conquer the primers in Italian. But he secured a phrase-book and a grammar, and paid for them in hard labor. With those crude implements, without a teacher, he determined to read that book. Only one friend, a young priest in St. Mark's Cathedral, gave him any word or look of encouragement. But his candle burned late, and the returning daylight took him to his book to study until time for breakfast. Then came the daily task as a messenger, or gondolier. Some weeks or months after he began his seemingly foolish problem he rushed into his mother's room at night, excited and noisy, shouting to her: "I can read that book! I can read that book!" There comes a moment in the life of every successful student of a foreign language when he suddenly awakens to the consciousness that he can think in that language. From that point on the work is always easy. It must have been a similar psychological change which came into Daniel's intellect. So sudden was it, so amazing the change, that the priest reported the case as a miracle, and the little circle of the poor people who knew the boy looked on him with awe. Consul-General Sparks, who represented the United States at Venice in 1848, wrote that "Manin often mentions his intellectual new birth, and his success in reading the life of Washington in English spurs him on in the difficult and dangerous undertakings connected with the efforts of Venice to get free."

When Daniel began to appreciate his ability to determine to do and to persevere, his ambition and hope brought to him larger views of life. He resolved to learn in other ways. He took up school books and mastered them thoroughly, and he became known as "a boy who works slowly, but what he does at all he does well." He soon found helpers among kind gentlemen and secured employment in a bookstall. The accounts of his persistence and his achievements are as thrilling and as fascinating as any finished romance. He managed to get a college education, recognized by Padua University; he studied law and was admitted to the bar when he was twenty-two years of age. The Austrian judges would not admit him to their courts, and it is said he visited his law-office regularly and daily for nearly two years before he had a paying client. But his strong will, shown in his perseverance in the presence of starvation, won the respect and love of the daughter of a wealthy patrician. They had been married but a short time when the Austrians confiscated the property of his father-in-law because of suspicions circulated concerning his secret connection with the "Americani." That patriotic secret society was called the "Carbonari" by the Austrians, and Manin became the leading spirit in the Venetian branch. His will seemed resistless. He refused the Presidency in 1832, when revolution shook the tyrannies of all Europe and Venice fell back under Austrian control. But in 1848 he was almost unanimously elected President of the "American Republic of Venice"; and in his second proclamation before the great siege began he issued a call for the election, using, as Consul-General Sparks records, the following language (as translated): "and until the election is held and the officers installed the following sections of the Constitution of the United States of America shall be the law of the City." He was determined to secure an "American republic" in Italy. He lived to see it in Venice. Statues of Daniel Manin are seen now in all the great cities of Italy; and when the statue was dedicated at Venice and a city park square named after him, he was called the father of the new kingdom of Italy. General Garibaldi said that when Manin made a draft of the Constitution he proposed for United Italy, he quoted the American Declaration of Independence. The general also said that Manin insisted the Government of Italy should be like the American Republic, and that it was difficult to convince Manin that a king—so called—could be as limited as a President. Even Mazzini, the extremist, and both Cavour and Gavazzi finally came to accept Manin's demands for freedom and equality as they were set forth in the Constitution of the American Republic. Manin did not live to see the final union, nor to see his son a general in the Italian army, but his vigorous will gave a momentum to freedom in Italy which is still pressing the people on to his noblest ideals. "What man has done man can do," and what Manin did can be done again in other achievements.

The normal reader never was anxious that the North Pole should be located, and he does not care now whether it has been discovered. Mathematicians and geographers may find delight in the solution of some abstract problem, but the busy citizen who seizes his paper with haste to see if Peary has found the North Pole has no interest in the spot. He would not visit the place if some authority would give him a thousand acres or present him with a dozen ice-floes. What the reader desires is to learn how the will power in those discoverers worked out through hair-breadth escapes, long winters, and starvation's pangs. It is a great game, and the world is a grand stand. The man with the strongest will attracts the admiration of the world. All the world which loves a lover also admires a hero, and a hero is always a man of forceful will. When we read of Louis Joliet and James Marquette in their terrible experience tracing the Mississippi River—Indians as savage as wild beasts, marshes, lakes, forests, mountains, burdens, illness, wounds, exhaustion, seeming failures—all testify to their sublime strength of purpose. Peter Lemoyne, Jonathan Carver, Captain Lewis, Lieutenant Clark, Montgomery Pike, General Fremont, Elisha Kent Kane, Charles Francis Hall, David Livingstone, Captain Cook, Paul Du Chaillu, and Henry M. Stanley carved their names deep in walls of history when differing from other men only in the cultivation of a mighty will.

Mary Lyon, the heroine of Mount Holyoke, used to quote frequently the saying of Doctor Beecher that he once had "a machine admirably contrived, admirably adjusted, but it had one fault; it wouldn't go!" while Catherine Beecher would retort that Miss Lyon had "too much go for so small a machine." But what a monumental triumph was the dedication of the first building of Mount Holyoke College at South Hadley, Massachusetts. Mrs. Deacon Porter wrote to Henry Ward Beecher: "I wish you could have seen Miss Lyon's face as the procession moved up the street. It was indeed the face of an angel." From that immortal hour when that little woman, peeling potatoes as her brother's housekeeper at Buckland, Massachusetts, suddenly determined to start a movement for the higher education of young women, she had written, had traveled, had begged, had given all her inheritance, had visited colleges and schools, going incessantly, working, praying, appealing, until the material embodiment of her martyr sacrifices was opened to women. All women in all countries are greatly in her debt. Men feel grateful for what the higher education of women has done for men. One cannot now walk over the embowered campus of Mount Holyoke College without meditating on what a forceful will of a frail woman, set toward the beautiful and good, can do within the severest limitations. Vassar, Wellesley, Smith, Bryn Mawr, and the thirty-five other colleges for women in Western and Southern states are the children of Mount Holyoke. One lone woman, one single will, a large heart! God sees her and orders His forces to aid her!

Richard Arkwright, Stephenson, and Edison in the pursuit of an invention, with stern faces and clenched teeth, work far into the morning. John Wesley, Whitfield, and the list of religious reformers from St. Augustine to Dwight L. Moody have been men of dynamic confidence in the triumph of a great idea. Neal Dow, Elizabeth Fry, and their disciples, urging on the cause of temperance with that motive force which they discovered in themselves, aroused the people wherever they went to assistance or to opposition. Fulton said, "I will build a steamboat." Cyrus Field said, "I will lay a telegraph cable to Europe." Sir Christopher Wren, imitating the builders of St. Peter's, said, "I will build the dome of St. Paul's Cathedral." General Washington said, "I will venture all on final victory," and General Grant said, "I will fight it out on this line." When Abraham Lincoln gave his eloquent tribute to Henry Clay in 1852 he said, "Henry Clay's example teaches us that one can scarcely be so poor but that, if he will, he can acquire sufficient education to get through the world respectably." To such men log cabins were universities. Daniel Webster decided, at the end of his day's work plowing a stony field in the New Hampshire hills, that he would be a statesman. Thomas H. Benton, when nearly all men supposed the wilderness unconquerable, decided to push the Republic west to the Rocky Mountains. Salmon P. Chase, from the time he ran the ferryboat on the Cuyahoga River, kept in his pocket-book a motto, "Where there is a will there is a way." Charles Sumner had a disagreeable habit of talking about himself and boasting of his learning. He was frankly told one day by James T. Fields that it was a "weakening trait." Mr. Sumner thanked Mr. Fields and told him that he had determined "to discontinue such foolish talk." "He fought himself," wrote Mr. Fields, "and he conquered." James G. Blaine, in college at Washington, Pennsylvania, saw a student who had been too devoted to football weeping over his failure to pass an examination. Warned by the failure of this student, James told his mother that he would not play another game of football while he was in college. He kept his resolution unbroken throughout the course. When James A. Garfield was earning his tuition as a bell-ringer at Hiram College he resolved that the first stroke of the bell should be exactly on the minute throughout the year. The president of the college stated that the people in the village set their clocks by that bell, and not once in the year was it one minute ahead or behind time. Grover Cleveland at eighteen was drifting about from one job to another, and men prophesied that he would be a disgrace to his "over-pious" father, who was a preacher. Mr. Cleveland said in a speech that, "like Martin Luther, I was stopped in my course by a stroke of lightning." It does not appear to what he referred, but it does appear that he decided firmly that he would choose some calling and stick to it. He decided upon the law, and was so fixed in his determination to know law that he stayed in his tutor's office three years after he had been admitted to the bar, and there continued persistently in his studies.

In a small town

in Western

Massachusetts—

IV

In a small town in western Massachusetts, forty years ago, a young, pale youth was acting as cashier of the savings bank. He was dyspeptic, acutely nervous, and often ill-natured. One day several large factories closed their doors, and the corporations to whom the bank had loaned money gave notice of bankruptcy. The president of the bank was in Europe and the people did not know that the bank was a loser by the failure. The cashier was almost overcome by the sense of danger, for he could not meet a run on the bank with the funds he had on hand. He entered the bank after a sleepless night, fearing that the people might in some way learn of the bank's responsibility. He was sleepy, faint, discouraged. An old farmer came in to get a small check cashed, and the glum cashier did not answer the farmer's usual salutation. His face was cloudy, his eyes bloodshot, and his whole manner irritating. He counted out the money and threw it at the farmer. The old man counted his money carefully and then called out to the cashier: "What's the matter? Is your bank going to fail?" When the farmer had left the bank the young cashier could see that his manner was letting out that which he wished to conceal. He then paced up and down the bank and fought it all out with himself. He determined he would be cheerful, brave, and strong. He forced himself to smile, and soon was able to laugh at himself for presenting such a ridiculous appearance. He met the next customer with a hearty greeting of good cheer. All the forenoon he grew stronger in his determination to let nothing move him to gloom again. About noon the daily Boston paper came and announced the possible failure of that bank. Almost instantly the news flew about town, and a wild mob assailed the bank, screaming for their money. But the cheerful cashier met them with a smile and made fun of their excitement. The eighteenth man demanding his money was an old German, who, seeing the cashier count out the money so coolly and cheerfully, drew back his bank-book and said: "If you have the money, we don't want it now! But we thought you didn't have it!" That suggestion made the crowd laugh, and in half an hour the crowd had left and those who had drawn their money in many cases asked the cashier to take it back. The cashier now is a most successful manufacturer and railroad director, stout-hearted and cheerful. He often refers to the fight he had that morning with his "insignificant, flabby little self."

To appreciate one's power at command is the first consideration. A man from Cooperstown, New York, visited St. Anthony Falls, Minnesota, in the early fifties of the last century and laughed loud and long at the ridiculous little mill which turned out a few bags of flour and sawed a few thousand feet of lumber. It was indeed ludicrous. He could think of no comparison except an elephant drawing a baby's tin toy. His laughter led to a heated discussion and investigation. An army officer at Fort Snelling, who was a civil engineer, was asked to make an estimate of the Mississippi River's horse-power at St. Anthony Falls. His report was beyond the civilian's belief. He said there was power enough to turn the wheels to grind out ten thousand barrels of flour a day and to cut logs into millions of square feet of board every hour. The estimate was below the facts, but was not accepted for ten years. Then was constructed the strong dam which built up the great city of Minneapolis and represents the finest and most vigorous civilization of our age. Nevertheless, there still runs to waste ten thousand horse-power. In the first paper-mill erected at South Hadley Falls, Massachusetts, the horse-power used was less than one hundred, yet an engineer employed by Mr. Chapin, of Springfield, to determine the possible power of the Connecticut River at that point reported it so great that unbelief in his figures postponed for a long time all the proposed enterprises. But one poor man, determined "to do something about it," promoted a system of canals which now so utilizes the water that a large city, manufacturing annually products worth many millions, draws from it comfort and riches. Massive as are the present works at Holyoke, regret is often expressed that so much of the water-power still goes over the mighty dam and ridicules the smallness of the faith of those who tried to harness it.

Such is the intellectual force in a young person's mind. It is reasonable to conclude that no mind ever did its very best, and that no will power was ever exerted continuously to its greatest capacity. But the first essential in the making of noble character is to gain a full appreciation of the latent or unused force which each individual possesses. When one without foolish egotism realizes how much can be done with his wasting energies, then he must carefully consider to what object he will turn his power. Great wills are often wasted on unworthy objects, and the strong current of the mind, which could be applied to the making of world-enriching machinery, is used to manufacture some unsalable toy. The mind is often compared to an electric dynamo. The figure is accurate. It is an automatic, self-charging battery which, when applied to worthy occupation or to a high purpose, distributes happiness, progress, and intelligence to mankind, and as a natural consequence brings riches and honor to the industrious possessor.

Forty years ago there was on the lips of nearly every teacher and father a fascinating story of a Massachusetts boy whose history illustrates forcibly the "power to will" which is latent in us all. I need not state the details of the life, as it is only the illustration which we need here.

A young fellow sat on a barrel at the door of a country grocery-store in a small village not far from Boston. He was the son of an industrious mechanic who had opened a small shop for making and repairing farm utensils, such as rakes, hoes, and shovels. But the son, encouraged by an indulgent mother, would not work. He gave way to cards, drink, and bad company. He would not go to school, and was a continual source of alarm to his parents, and he became the talk of the neighbors. He either was ill with a cough or pretended to fear consumption; the doctor's advice to set him at work in the open air was not enforced by his anxious mother. He was a fair sample of the many thousand young men seen now about the country stores and taverns. He had, however, the unusual disadvantage of having his board and clothing furnished to him without earning them. If he exercised his will, it was to turn it against himself in a determined self-indulgence. I heard him once refer to those days and quote Virgil in saying that "the descent to Avernus is easy."

One evening with his hands in his pockets he strolled up to the store and post-office to meet some other young men for a game of checkers. Under the only street lamp near the store a patent-medicine peddler had opened one side of his covered wagon and was advertising his "universal cure." The boy—then about nineteen years old—listened listlessly to the songs and stories, but was not interested enough to learn what was offered for sale. The vender of medicines held up a chain composed of several seemingly solid rings which he skilfully took apart. He then offered a dollar to any one who would put the rings together as they were before. The puzzle caught the eye and interest of the careless boy; as the rings were passed from one to another they came to him. He looked them over and said, "I can't do it," and passed them on. The Yankee peddler yelled at the boy, "If you talk like that you will land in the poorhouse!" The young fellow was cut to the heart with the short rebuke. He was inclined to answer hotly, but lacked the courage. After the other boys had had their chance to see the rings, he asked to examine them again; but he still saw no way to cut or open the solid steel and contemptuously threw them at the peddler and shouted, "You're fooling; that can't be done!" The smiling vender rolled the rings into a chain in an instant and, throwing it to the boy, said, sarcastically: "Take it home to your mother; she can do it!" The young fellow, ashamed, angry, and crushed, caught the chain and crept out of the crowd and went home, entering his room by the back stairs. He hated the peddler with a murderous passion, but despised himself and must have wept great tears far into the night. The next morning he sat on the side of his bed, gazing at the chain, long after his father had gone to work. That was a terrible battle! All who succeed must fight that battle to victory at some time, or life is a failure. He who conquers himself can conquer other men. He who does not rule himself cannot control other people. For the first time that boy was conscious of his lack of WILL. He was painfully ashamed. He could not again meet the boys, or the one girl who was at the post-office, unless he solved that riddle. It was far worse to him than the riddles of the ancient oracles or the questions of Samson had been to the ancients. No victory so glorious to any man as that when he rises over his dead self and can shout with unwavering confidence, I WILL. That young man's battle was furious and a strain on body and soul; he kept saying over and over again, "I will solve that riddle." He was sorely tempted by hunger, as he would not stop to eat. He determined to win out alone, and did not ask aid even of his mother. That night the rings fell apart in his hands and rolled on the floor. He had won! Life has few joys like that hour of victory. The rings had little value as pieces of steel, but his triumph over self was worth millions to him, and worth a thousand millions to his country.

The next morning his parents were surprised to see him the first one at the breakfast-table. He told of his solution of the puzzle, and said to his astonished but delighted parents that he had loafed around long enough and that he had determined to take hold and do things. He asked for an especially hard place in the shop, and entered that week on a noble, triumphant career, having few equals save those of like experience. His health became robust, his work became profitable, new business ideas were developed, and in a few years he controlled the inside business and far distanced all outside competitors. He said to his wife, "I will have a million dollars, and every dollar shall be a clean and honest dollar." In those days a million looked like a mountain of gold. But he secured the million and steadily raised the pay of his workmen. He became the sheik of the town, the father and adviser of every local enterprise. He was sent to Congress by a nearly unanimous vote. For eleven years he was a safe counselor of the administration at Washington and was a close friend and trusted supporter of President Lincoln.

One day in 1864 the Federal armies had been defeated by the Confederate forces and gloom shadowed the faces of the people. President Lincoln had a sleepless night—it looked like defeat and disunion. The danger was greatly increased by the abandonment of the scheme to hold California to the Union by building a railroad through the mountainous wilderness of the Sierra Nevada and Rocky Mountains. The chief engineer who surveyed the route said that it could not be done because of the great cost. Three great financiers had been consulted and refused to undertake the hopeless task. The great Massachusetts Senator told Mr. Lincoln that there was just one man who could do that gigantic feat. The Senator said to Lincoln: "If that Congressman makes up his mind to do it, and it is left to him, he will do it. He is a careful man, but he has a will which seems to be irresistible." President Lincoln sent for the Congressman and said: "A railroad to California now will be more than an army, and it will be an army—in the saving of the Union. Will you build it?" The Congressman asked for three weeks to think. Before the end of that time he asked the Secretary of War to take his card to President Lincoln, then in Philadelphia; on the card was written, "I will." What a startlingly fascinating story from real life is the history of that mighty undertaking. Now, when the traveler passes the highest point on that transcontinental railroad, 8,550 feet above the sea at Sherman, Wyoming, and lifts his hat before the monument erected to the memory of that civil nobleman and hero, he is paying his respect to the self-giving heart and mighty brain of the boy who conquered the three links.

It may not be necessary to multiply illustrations of this vital question, but no one who lived in the journalistic circles of Washington subsequent to the Civil War can forget the power and fame of that feminine literary genius who, as the Washington correspondent of theNew York Independent, wrote such brilliant letters. The fact that she bore the same name as the Congressman we have mentioned, though no relative of his, does not account for this reference to her. She was nearly thirty-three years old when a divorce and the breaking up of her home left her poor, ill, and under the cloud of undeserved disgrace. Her acquaintances predicted obscurity, daily toil with her hands, and a life of lonely sorrow. Poor victim of sad circumstances! She had but little education, and had been too full of cares to read the books of the day. Her start in the profession which she later so gracefully and forcibly adorned was the foremost topic in corners and cloakrooms at her largely attended literary receptions in Washington.

She had been told by those who loved her that a divorced woman would be shunned by all cultured women and be the butt of ridicule for fashionable men; and that as she must earn a living she should sew or embroider or act as a nurse. She certainly was too weak to wash clothes or care for a kitchen. But within her soul there was that yearning to do something worth while which seems given to almost every woman. Few women reach old age without feeling that somehow the great object of living has not been attained. The ambitions to which a man can give free wings, a woman must suppress or hide in deference to custom or competition. As yet she has seldom under our civilization seemed to do her best or accomplish the one great ideal of her heart and intellect. While she has the same God-given impulses, visions, and sense of power, she builds no cathedrals, spans no rivers, digs no mines, founds no nations, builds no steamships, and seldom appears in painting, sculpture, banking, or oratory. She is conscious of the native talent, sees the ideals, but must hide them until it is too late. But this woman from the interior of New York State was an exception; like Charlotte Brontë, she said, "I will write." Like the same great author, she had her rebuffs and returned manuscripts, and all the more since at that time women were unknown in the newspaper business. But her invariable answer to critics and discouraged friends was, "I will." When in 1883 she said, "I will," to the great editor who became her second husband, the President of the United States wrote a personal letter to say that, while he wished her joy, he could but admit that it would be a "distinct loss to humanity to have such a brilliant genius hidden by marriage."

In an automobile ride from Lake Champlain to New York I saw the city of Burlington, Vermont, with its university, where Barnes had said, "I will." At St. Johnsbury the whole city advertises Fairbanks, who said, "I will." At Brattleboro the hum of industry ever repeats the name of the boy Esty, who said, "I will"; at Holyoke, the powerful canals seem to reflect the faces of Chase and Whitney, who, when poor men, said, "I will." At Springfield the signs on the stores, banks, and factories suggest the young Chapin, who made the city prosperous with his "I will." At New Haven Whitney's determination stands out in great streets and university buildings.

Chicago, Denver, Los Angeles, New Orleans, Atlanta, Raleigh, Niagara, Pittsburg and a hundred American cities like them are the outcome of ideas with wills behind them in the heads of common men. If every man had in the last generation done all that it was in his power to do, what sublime things would stand before us now in architecture, commerce, art, manufactures, education, and religion. The very glimpse of that vision bewilders the mind. But the many will not to do, while the few great benefactors of the race will to do. My young friend, be thou among those who will with noble motives to do.

THE END

The Key To Success

By
Russell H. Conwell

The Key To Success

I

OBSERVATION — THE KEY TO SUCCESS

Years ago we went up the Ganges River in India. I was then a traveling correspondent, and we visited Argra, the sacred city of northern India, going thence to the Taj Mahal. Then we hired an ox team to take us across country twenty-two miles to visit the summer home of Ackba, the great Mogul of India. That is a wonderful, but dead city.

I have never been sorry that I traversed that country. What I saw and heard furnished me with a story which I have never seen in print.Harper's Magazine recently published an illustrated article upon the city, so that if you secure the files you may find the account of that wonderful dead city at Futtepore Sicree.

As we were being shown around those buildings the old guide, full of Eastern lore, told us a tradition connected with the ancient history of that place which has served me often as an illustration of the practical ideas I desire to advance. I wrote it down in the "hen tracks" of short-hand which are now difficult to decipher. But I remember well the story.

He said that there was a beautiful palace on that spot before the great Mogul purchased it. That previous palace was the scene of the traditional story. In the palace there was a throne-room, and at the head of that room there was a raised platform, and upon the platform was placed the throne of burnished gold. Beside the throne was a pedestal upon which rested the wonderful Crown of Silver, which the emperor wore when his word was to be actual law. At other times he was no more than an ordinary citizen. But when he assumed that crown, which was made of silver because silver was then worth much more than gold, his command was as absolute as the law of the Medes and Persians.

The guide said that when the old king who had ruled that country for many years died he was without heirs, leaving no person to claim that throne or to wear that Crown of Silver. The people, believing in the divine right of kings, were unwilling to accept any person to rule who was not born in the royal line. They wasted twelve years in searching for some successor, some relative of the late king. At last the people sank into anarchy, business ceased, famine overspread the land, and the afflicted people called upon the astrologers—their priests—to find a king.

The astrologers, who then worshiped the stars, met in that throne-room and, consulting their curious charts, asked of the stars:

"Where shall we find a successor to our king?"

The stars made to them this reply:

"Look up and down your country, and when you find a man whom the animals follow, the sun serves, the waters obey, and mankind love, you need not ask who his ancestors were. This man will be one of the royal line entitled to the throne of gold and the Crown of Silver."

The astrologers dispersed and began to ask of the people:

"Have you seen a man whom the animals follow, the sun serves, the waters obey, and mankind love?"

They were only met with ridicule. At last, in his travels, one gray old astrologer found his way into the depths of the Himalaya Mountains. He was overtaken by a December storm and sought shelter in a huntsman's cottage on the side of a mountain.

That night, as he lay awake, weeping for his suffering and dying people, he suddenly heard the howl of a wild beast down the valley. He listened as it drew nearer. He detected "the purr of the hyena, the hiss of the tiger, and the howl of the wolf." In a moment or two those wild animals sniffed at the log walls within which the astrologer lay. In his fright he arose to close the window lest they should leap in where the moonlight entered. While he stood by the window he saw the dark outline of his host, the huntsman, descending the ladder from the loft to the floor. The astrologer saw the huntsman approach the door as though he were about to open it and go out. The astrologer leaped forward, and said:

"Don't open that door! There are tigers, panthers, hyenas, and wolves out there."

The huntsman replied:

"Lie down, my friend, in peace. These are acquaintances of mine."

He flung open the door and in walked tiger, panther, hyena, and wolf. Going to the corner of his hut, the huntsman took down from a cord, stretched across the corner, the dried weeds which he had gathered the fall before because he had noticed that those weeds were antidotes for poisoned wild animals. Those poisoned animals had sniffed the antidote from afar and gathered at his door. When he opened that door they followed him to the corner of the hut, in peace with one another because of their common distress. He fed each one the antidote for which it came, and each one licked his hand with thanks and turned harmlessly out the door. Then the huntsman closed the door after the last one, and went to his rest as though nothing remarkable had happened.

This is the fabulous tradition as it was told me.

When the old astrologer lay down on his rug after the animals were gone, he said to himself, "The animals follow him," and then he caught upon the message of the stars and said, "It may be this huntsman is the king," but on second thought he said, "Oh no; he is not a king. How would he look on a throne of gold and wearing a Crown of Silver—that ignorant, horny-handed man of the mountains? He is not the king."

The next morning it was cold and they desired a fire, and the huntsman went outside and gathered some leaves and sticks. He put them in the center of the hut upon the ground floor. He then drew aside a curtain which hid a crystal set in the roof, which he had placed there because he had noticed that the crystal brought the sunlight to a focused point upon the floor. Then the astrologer saw, as that spot of light approached the leaves and sticks with the rising of the sun, the sticks began to crackle. Then the leaves began to curl, little spirals of smoke arose, and a flame flashed forth. As the astrologer looked on that rising flame, he said to himself:

"The sun has lit his fire! The sun serves him; and the animals followed him last night; after all, it may be that he is the king."

But on second thought he said to himself again: "Oh, he is not the king; for how would I look with all my inherited nobility, with all my wealth, cultivation, and education, as an ordinary citizen of a kingdom of which this ignorant fellow was a king? It is far more likely to be me."

A little later the astrologer desired water to drink, and he applied to the huntsman, and the huntsman said, "There is a spring down in the valley where I drink."

So down to the spring went the astrologer. But the wind swept down and roiled the shallow water so that he could not drink, and he wentback and complained of that muddy water. The huntsman said:

"Is that spring rebellious? I will teach it a lesson."

Going to another corner of his hut, he took down a vial of oil which he himself had collected, and, going down to the spring with the vial of oil, he dropped the oil upon the waters. Of course, the surface of the spring became placid beauty. As the astrologer dipped his glittering bowl into the flashing stream and partook of its cooling draught, he felt within him the testimony, "This is the king, for the waters obey him!" But again he hesitated and said, "I hope he is not the king."

The next day they went up into the mountains, and there was a dam holding back, up a valley, a great reservoir of water. The astrologer said, "Why is there a dam here with no mill?" And the huntsman said: "A few years ago I was down on the plains, and the people were dying for want of water. My heart's sympathies went out for the suffering and dying humanity, and when I came back here I noticed...."

I may as well stop here in this story and emphasize this phrase. He said, "When I came back here I noticed." This is the infallible secretof success. I wish you to be happy; I wish you to be mighty forces of God and man; I wish you to have fine homes and fine libraries and money invested, and here is the only open road to them. By this road only have men who have won great success traveled.

The huntsman said: "When I came back here I noticed a boulder hanging on the side of the mountain. I noticed it could be easily dislodged, and I noticed that it would form an excellent anchorage in the narrow valley for a dam. I noticed that a small dam here would hold back a large body of water in the mountain. I let the boulder fall, filled in for the dam, and gathered the water. Now every hot summer's day I come out and dig away a little more of the dam, and thus keep the water running in the river through the hot season. Then, when the fall comes on, I fill up the dam again and gather the waters for the next year's supply."

When the astrologer heard that he turned to the huntsman and said:

"Do mankind down on the plains know that you are their benefactor?"

"Oh yes," said he; "they found it out. I was down there a little while ago, selling the skins I had taken in the winter, and they came aroundme, kissed me, embraced me, and fairly mobbed me with their demonstrations of gratitude. I will never go down on the plains again."

When the astrologer heard that mankind loved him, all four conditions were filled. He fell upon his knees, took the horny hand of the huntsman, looked up into his scarred face, and said:

"Thou art a king born in the royal line. The stars did tell us that when we found a man whom the animals followed, the sun served, the waters obeyed, and mankind loved, he would be the heir entitled to the throne, and thou art the man!"

But the huntsman said: "I a king! Oh, I am not a king! My grandfather was a farmer!"

The astrologer said: "Don't talk about your grandfather. That has nothing to do with it. The stars told us thou art the man."

The huntsman replied: "How could I rule a nation, knowing nothing about law? I never studied law!"

Then the astrologer cut short the whole discussion with a theological dictum quoted from the ancient sacred books, which I will give in a very literal translation:

"Let not him whom the stars ordain to rule dare disobey their divine decree."

Now I will put that into a phrase a little more modern:

"Never refuse a nomination!"

When the huntsman heard that very wise decision he consented to be led down to the Juna Valley and to the beautiful palace. There they clothed him in purple. Then, amid the acclaim of happy and hopeful people, they placed upon his brow that badge of kingly authority—the Silver Crown. For forty years after that, so the old guide said to us, he ruled the nation and brought it to a peace and prosperity such as it had never known before and has never enjoyed since.

That wonderful tradition, so full of illustrative force, has remained with me all the subsequent years. When I look for a man to do any great work, I seek one having these four characteristics. If he has not all four he must have some of them, or else he is good for little in modern civilization.

II
WHO THE REAL LEADERS ARE

Among all of you who read this book I am looking for the kings and queens. I am looking for the successful men and women of the future. No matter how old you may be, you yet have life before you. I am looking for the leading men and women, and I will find them with these four tests. I cannot fail; it is infallible.

Some men, intensely American, will say:

"Oh, we don't have any kings or queens in this country."

Did you ever observe that America is ruled by the least number of people of any nation known on earth? And that same small number will rule it when we add all the women, as we soon shall, to the voting population. America is ruled by a very few kings and queens. The reason why we are ruled by so few is because our people are generally intelligent. "Oh," you will ask, "do you mean the political boss rule?" Yes. That is not a good word to use, because it is misleading. America is ruled by bosses, anyhow, and it will be so long as we are a free people. We do not approve of certain phases of boss rule, and so don't misunderstand me when I state that a very few persons govern the American people. In my home city, Philadelphia, for instance, nearly two millions of people are ruled by four or five men. It will always be so. Everything depends on whether those four or five men are fitted for the place of leaders or not. If they are wise men and good men, then that is the best kind of government. There is no doubt about it. If all the eighty or ninety millions of people in the United States were compelled to vote on every little thing that was done by the Government, you would be a long time getting around to any reform.

An intelligent farmer would build a house. Will he, as a farmer, go to work and cut out that lumber himself, plane it himself, shape it himself? Will he be the architect of the house, drive all the nails, put on the shingles, and build the chimney himself? If he is an intelligent man he will hire a carpenter, an architect, and a mason who understand their business, and tell them to oversee that work for him. In an intelligent country we can hire men who understand statesmanship, law, social economics, who love justice. We hire them as skilled people to do what we are not able to do. Why should all the people be all the time meddling with something they don't understand? They employ people who do understand it, and consequently, in a free nation a few specially fitted people will ever be allowed to guide. They will be the people who know better than we know what to do under difficult or important circumstances.

You are ruled by a few people, and I am looking for these few people among my readers. There are some women in this country who now have more influence than any known statesman, and their names are hardly mentioned in the newspapers. I remember once, in the days of Queen Victoria, asking a college class, "Who rules England?" Of course, they said, "Queen Victoria." Did Queen Victoria rule England? During her nominal reign England was the freest land on the face of the earth, and America not half as free if you go to the extremes of comparison. She was only a figurehead, and she would not even express an opinion on the Boer War. It was all left to the statesmen, who had really been selected by the Parliament to rule. They were the real rulers.

I am looking for the real kings, not the nominal ones, and I shall find the successful men and women of the future by the four tests mentioned in the old tradition of the Silver Crown. The first one is:

"Animals will follow them."

If a dog or cat tags your heels to-morrow remember what I am writing about it here. It is evidence of kingship or queenship. If you don't have a cat or dog or an ox or a horse to love you, then I pity you. I pity the animal the most, but you are also a subject of sympathy. Is there no lower animal that loves to hear your footstep, whines after your heels, or wags the tail or shakes the head at your door? Is there no cat that loves to see you come in when the house has been vacant? Is there no faithful dog that rises and barks with joy when he hears your key in the door? If you have none it is time you had one, because one of the important pathways to great success is along the line of what animal life can give to us of instruction and encouragement.

The time has come when a dog ought to be worth at least a thousand dollars. The time has come when a horse that now trots a mile in 2:05 or 2:06 ought to trot a mile in fifty-five seconds. That is scientifically possible. Now, where are your deacons and your elders and your class leaders that you haven't a horse in your city that will trot a mile in fifty-five seconds?

"Oh," says some good, pious brother, "I don't pay any attention to trotting-horses! I am too religious to spend time over them."

Is that so? Who made the trotting-horse? Who used the most picturesque language on the face of the earth, in the Book of Job, to describe him? Did you ever own a trotting-horse? Did you ever see a beautiful animal so well fed, so well cared for, trembling on that line with his mane shaking, his eyes flashing, his nostrils distended, and all his being alert for the leap? And did you hear the shot and see him go? If you did and didn't love him, you ought to be turned out of the church.

The time has come when a horse may be as useful as a university.

At Yale University, one day, I heard a professor of science tell those boys that a horse has within its body so much galvanic or electric force continually generated by the activities of life, that if that electricity could be concentrated and held to a certain point, a horse could stand still and run a forty-horse power electric engine. He went further than that and said that a man has within his living body sufficient continually generated electricity which, if it were brought to a point, might enable him to stand still and run a ten-horsepower electric engine. I went out of that class-room with a sense of triumph, thinking:

"There is going to be use, after all, for the loafers who stand on the corners and smoke!"

In Europe, some years ago, a sewing-machine was invented on which a lady put her bare feet, and her electric forces started the machine. This power does not yet run the machine strong enough to force the needle for real sewing. The only question is to get more of the electricity of that lady through the machine and secure the greater power. Then if a young man wants a valuable wife he must marry one "full of lightning."

The time is very near at hand when all the motive power of the world may be furnished by animal life. When they get one step further the greatest airships will go up and take with them a lap dog. The airship will require no coal, no oil, but just the electric force of that lap dog; and if they carry up enough to feed that dog he will furnish the power to run the motors. The great high seas of the air will be filled with machines run by lap dogs or the electricity of the aviator himself. It is not so far away as many of you may suppose, and it is the greatly needed improvement of this time, not so much for the purpose of the war, as for peace.

The time has come when an old hen may become a great instructor of the world. I would rather send my child to an old hen than to any professor I ever saw in my life. That old biddy which scratches around your door, or who cackles beside your fence, or picks off your flowers, knows more of some things than any scientific professor on the face of the earth. I wish I knew what that old hen does. But there are some professors who pretend to have a wonderful intellect, who say:

"I graduated from Leipsic or from Oxford or Harvard, and I have no time to observe a hen."

No time to notice a hen? My friend, did you ever try to talk with her?

"No, I did not; she has no language."

Didn't you ever hear her call the chickens and see them come? Didn't you ever hear her scold the rooster, and see him go? Well, a hen does have a real language, and it is time you scientific professors understood what that old biddy says.

"Oh, but," says the professor, "I have no time to spend with a hen! They are around the place all the time, but I never take any special notice of them. I am studying the greater things in the world."

"Won't you come into my study a minute, professor, and let me examine you? You have examined the boys long enough, now let me examine you.

"Bring all you know of science and all the scientific applications ever made, and all the instruments that are ever used, bring all that the world has ever discovered of chemistry. Come, and take in your hand a dove's egg, just the egg. Now, professor, will you tell the person who is reading this book where, in this egg, is now the beating heart of the future bird? Can you tell where it is?"

"Oh no, I cannot tell that. I can tell you the chemistry of the egg."

"No, I am not looking for that. I am looking for the design in the egg. I am looking for something more divinely mysterious than anything of chemistry. Now, professor, will you tell me where in that egg is the bony frame that next will appear?"

"No, I cannot tell you that."

"Where is the sheening bosom, and where the wings that shall welcome the sun in its coming?"

"No man can tell that," says the professor.

The professor is quite right. It cannot yet be told. Yet, in that egg is the greatest scientific problem with which the world has ever grappled—the beginning of life and the God-given design. In that egg is the secret of life. Professor, tell me where this life begins. The professor says, "No man can answer questions like that."

Then, until we can answer, we must take off our hats every time we meet a setting hen. For that old biddy knows by instinct more about it than any one of us. She knows directly, through her instinctive nature from God, something about the beginnings of life that we cannot understand yet.

The last time I saw Dr. Oliver Wendell Holmes, the grand poet of Massachusetts, he asked me to go out in his back yard and see his chickens. He told me they would answer to their names. But it turned out that they were like our children, and would not show off before company. But I haven't any doubt those little chickens still with the hen did answer to their individual names when she alone called them. I am sure that great man understood the hen and chickens as fully as Darwin did the doves.

It was a wonderful thing for science that men like Holmes and Darwin could learn so much from the hen. It reminds me of a current event in Doctor Holmes's own life, though the biographies do not seem to have taken notice of it. He and Mr. Longfellow were very intimate friends. They were ever joking each other like two boys, always at play whenever they met. One day, it is said, Doctor Holmes asked Mr. Longfellow to go down to Bridgewater, in Massachusetts, to a poultry show. He went; he was greatly interested in chickens.

Those two great poets went down to the poultry show, and as they walked up the middle passageway between the exhibits of hens and chickens they came to a large poster on which was a picture of a rooster. He had his wings spread and mouth open, making a speech to a lot of little chickens. It was such a unique picture that Mr. Longfellow called Doctor Holmes's attention to it, and said:

"There, you love chickens, you understand them. What do you suppose a rooster does say when he makes a speech to chickens like that?"

They went on, and Doctor Holmes was studying over it. Finally he turned around and said, "Go on, I will catch up with you." He went back to that poster, got up on a chair, took the tacks out of the top, turned in the advertisement at the top, above the picture, and then took his pencil and drew a line from the bill of the rooster that was making that speech up to the top. There he wrote what he thought that rooster was saying to those chickens. They say that he did not make a single correction in it, of line or word. He then went after Mr. Longfellow and brought the great poet back to see the poster. He had written these words, in imitation of Longfellow's "Psalm of Life":

Life is real, life is earnest!And the shell is not its pen;Egg thou art, and egg remainest,Was not spoken of the hen,

Art is long, and Time is fleeting,Be our bills then sharpened well,And not like muffled drums be beating,On the inside of the shell.

In the world's broad field of battle,In the great barnyard of life,Be not like those lazy cattle!Be a rooster in the strife!

Lives of roosters all remind us,We can make our lives sublime,And when roasted, leave behind usHen tracks on the sands of time.

Hen tracks that perhaps another Chicken drooping in the rain, Some forlorn and hen-pecked brother, When he sees, shall crow again.

Animal life can do much for us if we will but study it, take notice of it daily in our homes, in the streets, wherever we are.

III
MASTERING NATURAL FORCES

It has been demonstrated by science that the mentality and disposition of all kinds of animal life are greatly affected by what they eat. Professor Virchow, of Germany, took two little kittens and fed them on different foods, but kept them in the same environment. After three months he went in and put out his finger at one of those little kittens, and it stuck up its back and spit and scratched and drew the blood. It was savage. He put out his finger to the other kitten, fed on the other food, and it rubbed against his finger and purred with all the loveliness of domestic peace. What was the difference between the kittens? Nothing in the world but what they ate.

Now I can understand why some men swear and some women scratch. It is what they eat.

The universities of the world are now establishing schools of domestic science for the purpose of training people to understand the chemistry of digestion and the chemistry of cooking. Oh, there is an awful need of better cooks! Yet the fashionable aristocratic American lady thinks it is altogether beneath her dignity to cook a pie or pudding, or boil potatoes. How short sighted that is! The need of better cooks is great. How many a man fails in business because his wife is a poor cook. How many a student is marked down because of the bad biscuit in the boarding-house. Oh yes, and how many a grave in yonder cemetery would be empty still if there had been a good cook in that house.

I have grappled with an awful subject now—the need of better cooks. A man can't even be pious with the dyspepsia. The American lady, so called, who sits in the parlor amid the lace curtains and there plies her needle upon some delicate piece of embroidery, and commits the wonderful chemistry of the kitchen to the care of some girl who doesn't know the difference between a frying-pan and a horse-rake, is not fit to be called an American lady. Any fool could sit amid the curtains, but it takes a giant mind to handle the chemistry of the kitchen. If women forsake that throne of power, men must take it, or our civilization must cease.

But I will not follow this thought into the thousands of discoveries animals suggest, because, in this wonderful tradition, the real king was not only followed by animals, but "the sun served him, and the waters obeyed him." Now I can combine those two thoughts for illustration, using the wonderful locomotive which draws our railway trains. The locomotive has within it the coal, which is the carbon of the sun. Thus the sun serves man by heating the water; and there is the water changing to steam and driving the piston-rods over the land, obeying man.

We need so much to travel faster than we do now. I saw a man not long ago who said he did not like to travel a mile a minute in a railway train. If you don't go faster than a mile a minute ten years from now you will feel like that old lady who got in a slow train with a little girl. The conductor came through and asked for a ticket for the little girl, and the old lady said:

"She is too young to pay her fare."

"No," said the conductor. "A great girl like that must pay her fare."

"Well," the mother replied, "she was young enough to go for nothing when we got in this train."

You will feel like that if you don't travel faster than a mile a minute ten years from now. The time is soon coming when, in order to go from Philadelphia to San Francisco, you will get in the end of a pipe or on a wire, and about as quick as you can say "that" you will be in San Francisco. Is that an extravagant expression? The time draws nigh when you won't say that is an extravagant expression. As I am writing this a company to lay that long-contemplated pneumatic tube from New York to Boston is being formed. They have been fighting in the courts over the right to lay it. When they finish it you can put a hundredweight of goods in the New York end of it, and it will possibly land in Boston in one minute and fifty-eight seconds. Now, then, what is to hinder making a little larger pipe and putting a man in and sending him in one minute and fifty-eight seconds? The only reason why you cannot send them with that lightning speed is for the same reason, perhaps, that the Irishman gave when he fell from a tall building and they asked, "Didn't the fall hurt you?" "No, it was not the falling that hurt me, it was the stopping so quick." That is all the difficulty there is in using now those pneumatic tubes for human travel.

We need those inventions now. We are soon going to find the inventors. Will you find them graduating from some university, or from some great scientific school at Harvard, Yale, Oxford, or Berlin? It may be. I would not say, while presiding over a university myself, that you would not find such people there. Perhaps you will.

But come back in history with me a little way and let us see where these men and women are to be found. Go into northern England, and go down a coal shaft underground two miles, and there is a young man picking away at a vein of coal a foot and a half thick. His hair sticks out through his hat, his face is besmirched, his fingers are covered with soot. Yet he is digging away and whistling. Is he a king? One of the greatest the world has ever seen. Queen Victoria, introducing her son, who has since been king, to that young man, said to him:

"I introduce you, my son, to England's greatest man."

What! This poor miner, who has never been to school but a few months in his life? While he had not been to a day school, he had been learning all the time in the university of experience, in the world's great university—every-day observation. When such a man graduates he gets the highest possible degree—D.N.R.—"Don't Need Recommends." Let us go in the mine and ask the miner his name.

"Young man, what is your name?"

"Stevenson."

The inventor of the locomotive itself! Oh, where are thy kings, oh, men? They may be in the mine, on the mountain, in the hovel or the palace, wherever a man notices what other people have not seen. Wherever a man observes in his every-day work what other people have not noticed, there will be found the king.

Are any of my readers milkmen? Are you discouraged when the brooks freeze up in the winter? Now, there was a milkman in West Virginia, not many years ago, who went to the train every morning with the milk from the farm, and while they were putting the milk in the car he studied the locomotive standing in the station.

"What do you know about a locomotive?"

"Oh, I don't know anything about it."

Is that so? You have seen and ridden after them all your lifetime, and you have seen them standing in the station, you have looked at the immense structure with some respect, but you don't know anything about it—and then you expect to be a successful man! That young manbecame interested in the locomotive, and while he stood around there he watched it, measured it, asked the engineer questions about it. One day the engineer, seeing he was interested, took him down to the switch and showed him how to put on the steam, and how to shut it off, and how to reverse the engine, ring the bell, operate the whistle, and all about it, and he was delighted. He went home and made draftings in the evenings of the locomotive.

Two years after that the same train ran on the siding and the engineer and fireman went into a house to get their breakfast, leaving the locomotive alone—waiting for the snow to be shoveled off the track which had rolled down the mountain. While they were absent a valve of the engine accidentally opened. It started the piston, and the engine began to draw out the train on to the main track, and then it began to go down the fearful grade at full speed. The brakeman went out on the rear platform, caught hold of the wheel brake in order to slow down the train. When he saw the engineer and fireman at the top of the hill swinging their arms as though something awful had happened, the brakeman shouted:

"There is the engineer and fireman, both of them, up there. We will all be killed!"

The people fainted and screamed, and the cry went to the second car, and then to the baggage car, and that milkman was there. He ran to the side-door to leap, but saw that it would be certain death. Then, with the help of the baggage-man he clambered over the tender, reached the engineer's place, and felt around for the lever in the smoke. When he discovered it he pressed it home. Then reversed the engine. It was a wonder those cylinder heads held. But with an awful crack the driving wheels stopped on the track, shot fire through the snow as they began to roll back against the ongoing train, the momentum still pushing it on. It shook the train until every pane of glass was broken. When it came to a stop the passengers climbed out to ascertain who stopped the train. They discovered that this young man had done it, and saved their lives, and they thanked him with tears.

A stockholder in the railroad company, an old man nearly eighty years of age, was on the train. He went into the stockholders' meeting that night and told the story of his narrow escape on that train. Since then that milkman has been one of the richest railroad owners in the world.

What do you suppose has become of the other milkmen who went at the same time to the same place and sat on the edge of the platform and swung their feet? What has become of them?

Ask the winds that sweep down from the Alleghany mountains — where are the other milkmen? The winds will answer, "They are going to the pump there still."

It was ever the same. Wherever you look, success in any branch of achievement depends upon this ability to get one's education every day as one goes along from the events that are around us now. The king is found wherever a person notices that which other men do not see.

IV
WHOM MANKIND SHALL LOVE

The great scientific men—and we need more—often are not given the full credit that is due them because they have not "graduated" from somewhere. It seems to me there is a feeling in these later days for creating an aristocracy among the men who have graduated from some rich university. But that does not determine a man's life. It may be a foolish tyranny for a little while, but nevertheless every man and woman must finally take the place where he and she are best fitted to be, and do the things that he and she can do best, and the things about which he and she really know. Where they graduated, or when, will not long count in the race of practical life.

We need great scientific men now more than we ever needed them before. Where are you going to find them? We won't find them where that scientific man came from who invented an improvement upon the cuckoo clock. His clock, instead of saying, "Cuckoo, cuckoo, cuckoo," when it struck the hour, said, "I love you! I love you! I love you!" That man left the clock at home with his wife nights while he was around at the club, thinking that would be sufficient protestation of his love. Yet any man knows you cannot make love by machinery. That was only a so-called scientific idea.

I read not long ago that a great scientific man said that "love and worship are only the aggregate results of physical causes." That is not true. Love and worship are something beyond physical causes. Educated men ought to know better than to say anything like that.

There are many valuable things that every man knows until he has unlearned them in a university.

There is danger that a man will get so much education that he won't know anything of real value because his useless education has driven the useful out of his mind. It is like a dog I owned when a boy. He was a very good fox dog. One day I thought I would show him off before the boys. We let the fox out at the barn door, which was open just far enough for the dog to see the fox start. Then he began whining and yelping to get out. I ran out and dropped some red pepper where the dog was likely to follow the fox over the hill. Then I went back and opened the door. The dog rushed out after the fox, but soon began to take in the red pepper. Then he began to whine and yelp—and stopped, whirled around, and, rushing down to the brook, put his nose under the water. From the time he graduated from that pepper university he never would follow a fox at all. He had added education in the wrong direction, and so it is often with these scientific men.

Do you know that the humblest man, whatever his occupation, really knows instinctively certain things better for not having been to school much? It is so easy to bias the mind.

When the boy comes to learn geometry the teacher will say: "Two parallel lines will never run together." The boy may look up and ask, "What is the use of telling me that?" Every man knows that two parallel lines will never run together. But how does he know it? It is born with him. His natural instincts tell that to him. It is what we call "an axiom"—a self-evident truth. It is above argument and beyond all possible reasoning. We know that "two halves are equal to the whole"! You know that when you cut an apple in half the two halves are equal to the whole of it. You tell that to a geometry class, and they say: "I know that. Everybody knows it." Of course everybody does, because it is a natural scientific fact that you cannot reasonably question.

Ask a man, "Do you know that you exist?" He looks with astonishment and says: "Certainly! Don't I know that I am? I know that I am here, that this is me, that I am not Mrs. Smith or some one else?"

Of course you do. But how do you know it? By a God-given instinct that came into the world with you.

No scientist or school on earth could disprove that, or prove it, either. It is a self-evident fact. I know that I am an intelligent personal identity, and that I dwell in this body in some mysterious way. I know that is my hand, but what I possess is not me. I know by an instinct infallible that I am a spiritual being, separate from this material. You know that. No scientist can prove or disprove it. It is a fact we all know. I know that I can never die, and you know it unless you have gotten educated out of it. It is in your very life; it is a part of your original instinct.

When some graduate of some great university shall come to you, young man, and say, "I can prove to you that the Bible is not true," or, "I can prove to you that your religion is false," you can say to him: "You are nothing but an educated fool. Because the more you have studied the less truth you seem to know."

It is only one's own personal self that can know his own religious instincts. It is only himself that can know whether he is in spiritual relation to God or not. No education on earth can overturn the fact, although wrong study may confuse the mind.

When a man comes to me, with his higher education, to overturn religion, it reminds me of what Artemus Ward said to that lordly graduate of Oxford and Cambridge. This man told Ward that he was disgusted with his shows. Artemus Ward asked him, "What do you know about these shows?" and he said: "I know everything about them. I graduated from two universities." Then Artemus Ward said, "You remind me of a farmer in Maine who had a calf that stole the milk of two cows, and the more milk he got the greater calf he was." Such is the effect sometimes of education on religious life—the more mental education of some kind which you get the less you may know about your natural religious instincts.

There is a great need to-day, and prayers go up to heaven now for men and women whom mankind shall love—love because they are great benefactors; love because, while they are making money or gaining fame or honor for themselves, they are blessing humanity all the way along. I must not argue now. I will illustrate, because you can remember the illustrations and you might forget an argument.

There is a great need for artists. There never was such a need in the progress of Christian civilization as there is now for great painters. All these walls ought to be covered with magnificent paintings teaching some great divine truth, and every school-house, yes, every barn, ought to have some picture upon it that will instruct and inspire. All our children seek to go to the moving pictures, and that shows what an agency there is in pictures for the instruction of mankind. We need artists by the thousands. It is not a surprise to me that a New York man is getting a salary of $35,000 a year for moving-picture work because "he notices something other people have not seen." It is no surprise that a great store in that city pays an advertising man $21,000 a year salary. He can see what the rest of the public does not see.

We need great artists, hundreds of them. Where are you going to find them? You will say "at the art school, in the National Gallery in London, or at the Louvre in Paris, or in Rome." Well, it may be that you will. But it is an unfortunate thing for your theory that one of the greatest painters in America painted with a cat's tail. It is another enlightening thing that the man who received the highest prize at the World's Fair in Chicago for a landscape painting never took "a lesson" in color or drawing in his life.

But that doesn't argue against lessons nor against schools or universities. Don't misunderstand me in this. I am only making emphatic my special subject.

He took the highest prize and never went to an art school in his life. If he had attended school the teacher might have tried to show him something and thus weakened his mind. The teacher in a school who shows a child anything that that child could work out for himself is a curse to that child. It is an awful calamity for a child to be under the control of a too kind-hearted teacher who will show him everything.

One of the greatest artists was Charlotte Brontë. She was a wonderful little woman, and I like little women. Did you ever read Longfellow's poem on "Little Women"? It always reminds me so much of Charlotte Brontë. One day he showed me the poem, and I asked him why he did not print it in his book, and he replied, "I don't think it is worth while." Since his death they have given it first rank, and I will quote one verse:

As within a little rose we find the richest dyes,As in a little grain of gold much price and value lies,And as from a little balsam much odor doth arise,So in a little woman there's a gleam of paradise.

Charlotte Brontë was one of those wonderful, wiry, beautiful little cultivated combinations of divine femininity which no man can describe. She had a younger brother on her hands, and when a young woman has a younger brother on her hands if she has a beau, she has her hands full. This younger brother was dull of brains, clumsy of finger and unfitted to be an artist. But his sister was determined he should be a painter, and took him to the shore, to the village and the woods, and said, "Notice everything, and notice it closely." Finally, he did secure a second prize. Then his little sister threw her arms about her brother's neck and kissed him, and thanked him for getting that prize. That is just like a woman! I never could understand a woman. Of all the mysterious things that the Lord ever put together, a woman is the most mysterious. Charlotte Brontë was like an old lady I used to know up in my native town who thanked her husband, with tears, for having brought up a flock of sheep which she herself fed every morning through the winter before he was out of bed.

Finally, Charlotte Brontë's younger brother became dissipated and died, and then her father died, and when we ministers get to be old we might as well die. She was left without means of support. But when she told her friends, they said: "You have a college education, Charlotte. Why don't you write something?" We now find that the first thing she wrote was "Jane Eyre," the wonderful story for which she at last received $38,000. Queen Victoria invited that humble girl to her palace at Windsor because of her marvelous genius.

How came she to write a book like that? Simply because she had noticed so closely, for her brother's sake, that from the nib of her pen flowed those beautiful descriptions as naturally as the water ripples down the mountain-side. That is always so. No man ever gives himself for others' good in the right spirit without receiving "a hundredfold more in this present time."

I will go one step farther with this thought. We do need great painters, but we don't want more painters like that man who painted the Israelites coming out of Egypt, representing them with muskets on their shoulders with U.S. on the butts.

But more than artists we need great musicians. There is an awful need of music. We have too much noise, but very little real music. Did you ever think how little you have? Do you suppose a true musician is simply a man who roars down to low B and squeals to high C? What an awful need there is of the music which refines the heart, brightens the mind; that brings glory and heaven down to men. I have not the space here to expand upon that thought—the awful need of humanity for real music. But we don't get it. I do not know why it is. I am not able to explain. But perhaps I can hint at what music is.

At Yale I had to earn my own living, and that is why, for these forty-four years, I have been lecturing exclusively to help young men secure their college education. I arose at four o'clock and worked in the New Haven House from four to eight to get the "come backs" from the breakfast table so that my brother and I could live. Some days, however, I digged potatoes in the afternoon, and taught music in the evening, although the former was my proper occupation. Sometimes my music scholars would invite me in to play something to entertain their company, and I noticed the louder I played the louder they talked. I often said, "What a low standard of musical culture there is in New Haven!" But I learned something after I left college. I learned I was not a musician.

Had I been a musician they would have listened. That is the only test of real music. There is no other.

If you sing and every one whispers, or you play and every one talks, it is because you are not a musician. I dare tell it to you here, when I would not dare say it to you individually if we were alone. There is no person on earth who gets so many lies to the square inch as a person who drums on a piano.

What is music? Music may be wholly a personal matter and be called music. I remember Major Snow, of my native town, who used to listen to the filing of the saw at the sawmill. How that did screech and scratch until it hurt to our toes! We asked the old major why he went down to the mill Saturday, when he could go any other day. He said: "Oh, boys, you do not understand it. When I was young I worked in a sawmill and I come down here to hear them file that saw. It reminds me of the good old days. It is music to me." He was "educated up" to that standard where filing of a saw was music to him, and so men may be educated in all manner of ways in so-called music. But it is not the real music.

What is true music? I went to a beautiful church in New York to exchange with the pastor, and an officer of the church came down the aisle as I walked in and said to me, "Sir, the choir always opens the service." They did; they opened it! I sat down on the pulpit sofa and waited an embarrassingly long time for something to be done up there. The choir roosted on a shelf over my head. The soprano earned $4,000 a year, and I was anxious to hear her. Soon I heard the rustle of silk up there, and one or two little giggles. Then the soprano began. She struck the lowest note her cultivated voice could possibly touch, and then she began to wind, or rather, corkscrew, her way up and up and up, out of sight—and she stayed up there. Then the second bass began and wound his way down, down, down—down to the Hades of sound—and he stayed down there.

Now, was that music? Was it worship? Why, if I had stood in that sacred place and positively sworn at the people it would not have been greater sacrilege than that exhibition up on that shelf! Do you think the living God is to be worshiped by a high-flying, pyrotechnic, trapeze performance in acoustics? Neither worship nor music was there. Music does not consist of a high-flying circus trapeze performance in acoustics.

What is music? Music is such a combination of sound as moves the heart to holier emotions, quickens the brain to brighter thoughts, and moves the whole man on to nobler deeds. That is music. Nothing else is music. You can only find out whether you are a musician or not by taking notice, while you sing, whether you hold the attention of the people, and whether you influence their memory and their after character.

V
NEED OF ORATORS

We need great orators. The need is something alarming. I am often called to lecture at the Chautauquas and the lyceums, and the committees often urge me to recommend some man or woman who will fill a place on the public platform. They offer marvelous rewards for those who will do that well. There are no men or women alive, not one known in our land to-day, who could be called a great orator. When I began to lecture, fifty-eight years ago, there were Henry Ward Beecher, Wendell Phillips, George William Curtis, Edward Everett, the greatest orator of his day—and John B. Gough. I esteem it a great honor to have been induced by Mr. Gough to go on the lecture platform. They are all gone, and no successors have appeared.

Liberty and oratory have ever gone together, and always will, hence the need of oratory is especially pressing now.

Why don't we have orators? The editors say "because the newspaper has come in and goes into every home, and a man on Sunday will read a better sermon in his newspaper than ever was delivered, and will save paying the minister and having trouble with the choir." Now, that time will never come. You will never get along without real orators, no matter how many newspapers you may have. I respect the press. I have had something to do with its work in my lifetime. I have worked upon and owned a daily newspaper. But I must say that there is something, after all, in the shake of a living man's finger, something in the flash of his eye, something in the stamp of his foot, but vastly more in his mesmeric power, which no cold type will ever express! You never can fully express the living man in cold lead.

Why don't we have great orators? I don't think the newspapers are in the way. But other people say to me. "It is the injurious effect of the modern school of elocution, which is now called 'the school of oratory.'" It has only been a few years since all these elocutionary schools changed their names to "schools of oratory" and consequently damaged the prospect of our country. The school of elocution may not be a school of oratory at all. It may be a hindrance to oratory; it depends on what the teaching is. There is a wide difference between elocution and real oratory. Elocution is an art of expression, which every teacher has, and he teaches his own art. But oratory is the great science of successful speech. The man who gets what he pleads for is an orator, no matter how he calls. If you call a dog and he comes, that is oratory. If he runs away, that is elocution!

Why don't we have greater orators? These schools of elocution remind me of an incident which occurred about seventeen years ago. I don't believe I will hurt any one's feelings now by mentioning it. The professor of elocution was sick one day, and the boys came after me. They wanted me to come because the teacher was away, and I resolved to go and entertain that class and let it pass for a recitation. Professors often do that. When I came into the class-room, I said to the boy on the front seat: "What was the last lesson you had in elocution?" One of the boys said:

"Peter Piper, pickle-picker, picked six pecks of pickled peppers;If Peter Piper, pickle-picker, picked six pecks of pickled peppers,Where are the six pecks of pickled peppers which Peter Piper picked?"

That is "lip exercise" in elocution. I said to that young man, "I will not teach elocution. But I wish you would come up and deliver that to this class just as you would to an audience." The boy came up and put his toes together, and his hands by his side, for he had not reached the study of gesture. He yelled very rapidly and loudly:

"Peter Piper, pickle-picker, picked six pecks of pickled peppers;If Peter Piper, piping, picked six pecks of pickled peppers,Where are the pecks of pickled peppers which Peter Piper picked?"

It was elocution, but it was not oratory. I had trouble in getting up another boy, but I finally did. He thought that oratory consisted entirely in elocutionary "inflections," so he delivered it:

"Peter Piper picked six pecks of pickled peppers;If Peter piping picked a peck of pickled peppers,Where's the peck of pickled peppers Peter Piper picked?"

(With marked raising and lowering of the voice.)

It sounded like an old rooster in the barn in the morning. But being elocution, it was not oratory.

But the most illustrative and most absurd speech I ever heard was by a visitor in that class that day. He was sitting over near the aisle, and one of the students came and whispered to me: "That young man has graduated from an Eastern school of elocution, and he is going to act the heavy parts in tragedy upon the stage. He is a great elocutionist, and won't you get him to recite something to the class?" I fell into the trap, and went down to the young man, and said: "I understand you are an elocutionist. Will you come up and recite something for the class?"

As soon as he looked up at me I saw by his eyes there was something the matter with his head. I do not know just what, but things have happened since that make it no unkindness to refer to him the way I do. I said: "Please come up and recite something," and he replied: "Shall I recite the same thing the young men have been reciting?" I said, "You don't need to do that; take anything." He left his gold-headed cane—the best part of him—on the floor, and then he came up to the platform and leaned on the table and said to me: "Shall I recite the same thing the young men have been reciting?" I said: "You can if you wish. You are perfectly free to take anything you choose. The professor is away, anyhow. When the cat is away the mice will play."

Then he began to prepare himself for that recitation. I never saw such behavior in my life. He pulled up his sleeves, brushed back his hair, shook himself, moved the table away forward, and I slid far back by the door and left the platform open, for I didn't know what he was going to do next. Then he gave the selection:

"Peter Piper picked a peck of pickled pepper-r-rs;If Peter Piper, piping piper, picked a peck of pickled pepper-r-r-rs,Where's the peck of pickled pepper-r-r-rs Peter Piper pickle-picker-r-r picked?"

He rolled in a flutter the letter "r" in each line. That class looked up with awe, and applauded until he repeated it. It was still elocution, but it was not oratory. He thought that oratory consisted of rolling the "r's" and rolling himself. That is not oratory.

Where do they learn oratory? They learn it in the old-fashioned schoolhouse, from that old hen at the kitchen door, in some back office, in some hall, or some church where young men or women get together and debate, saying naturally the things they mean, and then take notice of the effects of what they debate upon, the conviction or after action of those who listen. That is the place to observe. You musttake notice if you are to be a great orator.

The greatest orator of the future will be a woman. It has not been two months since the management of a women's Chautauqua said, "We could give $40,000 a year to any woman who will be a natural woman on the platform." They would make money at $40,000 a year if they hired a woman who would be a real woman. The trouble is that when women get on the platform they try to sing bass or try to speak as a man speaks. And there is such a need for women orators now! I get provoked about it when I think. Why isn't there a great woman orator like Mrs. Livermore now when she is needed so much?

VI

WOMAN'S INFLUENCE

If women vote they will be of little account unless they are leaders. It is of no special advantage to the voter to ignorantly put a piece of paper in a box. But it is of great account to influence ten thousand votes. That is what women must do if they are going to exercise their right under suffrage—they must be the influence behind the throne, not merely a voter.

When I was a boy in the district school a substitute teacher came in, and we all loved that little woman. We would do anything she asked us to do. One day that substitute teacher, who could not get a first-class certificate, copied a verse of a poem and asked me to read it:

If you cannot on the oceanSail among the swiftest fleet:Rocking on the mighty billows,Laughing at the storms you meet.

She asked me to read it once, and then she turned the paper over and said, "Now, Russell, repeat it." I said, "I have not learned it by heart." Said she: "Don't learn it by heart. I will try again." So she wrote the second verse:

If you are too weak to journeyUp the mountain steep and high.

Then she said to me, "Now, Russell, read it through once, and notice carefully each word, and don't look back at a word a second time." I know not now why she demanded that; I have looked in many books of psychology and in many places to find out. I have no explanation of this, and I ask you to think for me, for this is the fact. I took the second verse and read it through as she told me to do. Then she turned it over and said, "Please repeat it." I said, "I cannot repeat it; I have not learned it by heart." She replied: "Don't you say that again. Just shut your eyes and make a mental effort to see those verses, and then read it."

I shut my eyes and said, "Oh, it is all dark." Then she seemed very much disturbed and said: "Now, Russell, don't say that. Won't you try to do what I ask you to do?"

I thought the little woman was going to cry, so I said, "Yes, I will do the best I can." She said, "Shut your eyes again and make a determined effort, with your eyes shut, to see that poetry just as though it were right before you." I shut my eyes and made that effort, and saw it as distinctly as though I had held it before my open eyes. So long as my eyes were shut I could see the two verses, and I read it all through, word for word, and I read it backward, word for word, to the beginning.

I thought I had seen a ghost. I went home and told my father what had happened, and he rushed down from the pasture to the school-house and said to the teacher:

"If you indulge again in your foolish superstitions you will never teach in that school-house again."

It must have been uncomfortable for her, and her secret went down to the grave with her, as far as I know. Yet what would I not give if I could place before the world now what that little girl knew. All our educational institutions, for which I have labored all these years, would be as nothing compared with that one secret if I could give it to you — that secret of being able to look upon a scene and shut's one's eyes and bring it all back again, study it in detail.

I have not had great personal power in that line. But I have seen a man who would take a column of the morning paper and read it down, and hand me the paper and read it through with his eyes shut and scarcely make a mistake. I do not know that I ever saw any one who was infallible, but rarely would he make a mistake. Often he could tell me where the comma, semi-colon, and other marks of punctuation were.

I do not believe there is a normal child who is not mentally capable of that power when he has a teacher who understands how to develop it. That little teacher, who held only a second-class certificate, knew more about psyhology than many of the greatest men who preside over great institutions.

In the Alps some years ago was Professor Slayton, a native of Brighton, England. He was one of the nation's best botanists. His wife died and he was left with a little child between five and six years of age. They boarded at the Hotel Des Alps, in the Chamouni Valley. One morning he took his little girl up to the Mer-de-Glace, and then he told her to run back to the hotel, saying he would return to her in the evening.

She bid her father good-by and saw him go up Mont Blanc into the forest, and she ran back. He did not return in the evening, and she sat up all night and worried, and early in the morning she ran out from the hotel and ran up the stream to the path she had seen her father take. Then, running across, she started climbing up the side of the great snow-capped mountain. She came suddenly to a place where the path ran around along a projecting precipice, two hundred and eighty feet in the perpendicular, around a promontory of rock that set a few feet back. When she came to that spot her feet slipped upon the snow on the glare ice, and she slid down and down over the edge so far that her fingers just caught in the moss on the edge and one foot rested on about an inch projection of the rock.

As she hung there she screamed, "Papa!" Her father heard that cry. He was down in the valley so far that he could not see her, but he could hear her voice. He recognized it, and he felt there was an awful need of him—"humanity called to him." He ran across the valley and up the path. On the way there was a tree near which he had previously noticed there was an ax. He pulled out the ax and ran on to a tree where he had previously observed there was a rope which the coal-burners had long used to let coal down from the cliff. He clipped the rope with the ax, threw away the ax, and, tying the rope around him as he had noticed the guides do who take travelers over the "sea of ice," he ran on, until suddenly he came to the spot where his little girl had slipped. He could see the parting in her hair twenty feet down, and all was glare ice between. His heart must have stopped beating. But he suddenly shouted:

"Papa's come. Hold on tight!"

She screamed, "I cannot hold on any longer!"

He turned and threatened her. Oh, ye parents, whosoever you may be, you may save your own son or daughter from a physical or moral death by training them to obey when they are young. Her fingers tightened again, and he threw the rope around the butt of a tree he hadnoticed, and let himself rapidly down over that ice. He tried to get hold of his little child's hands, but they had melted deep into the moss, and he let himself down beside her and caught hold of her dress and pulled her to him.

Both were hanging from the edge of the cliff, and the end of the rope was in his hand, and his hand on the ice. He tried to pull himself up, but the rope would not give an inch, and then he tried to push his little girl up, but with frozen fingers she could not climb.

There they hung in the high Alps, alone! Will he fall on the jagged rocks and be crushed to death? No, he will not fall, because he is a king. He has used his every-day observation, though he is a graduate of a university. He had noticed something more—he had observed how the dogs howl when they find perishing travelers. Those St. Bernard dogs, whenever they find a dead body or a man laying insensible, will always howl in one peculiar way. Those dogs know more about acoustics than an architect. How do they know? God told them. When a dog utters that cry it can be heard for miles and miles. The professor imitated the call of the dog, and when it rang down the valley the coal-burners heard it and the wood-choppers heard it. They said:

"That is a dog, and a dog never howls like that unless he has found a dying man." So, throwing down their axes and guns, and running over the snows toward the sound of the call, they suddenly came to the spot. They caught hold of the rope and one of them slid down rapidly and seized the little girl's arm and passed her up, and then caught hold of the professor's arm and lifted him, while the others pulled upon the rope. Thus they dragged him up. The professor fell on the snow-drift and fainted dead away.

But he was a king. He heard humanity's cry, and when he heard it he knew where the ax was. He had used his every-day study in such a way that he knew where the old rope was, and knew how to tie it, and he knew how to call for help. Whenever you find on earth a successful man or woman you will always find it is a man or woman who hears humanity's call, and who has so used his every-day means of observation that he knows where the weapons are with which to fight those battles, or where the means are with which to bring men relief.

I could not better put into your minds that professor's feelings than by a quotation of an English phrase which he printed in English on his scientific books, though the books were published in French:

We live for those who love us,For those who know us true;For the heavens that bend above us,For the good that we can do.For the wrongs that lack resistance,For each cause that needs assistance,For the future in the distance,For the good that we can do.

www.ingramcontent.com/pod-product-compliance
Lightning Source LLC
Chambersburg PA
CBHW081203020426
42333CB00020B/2613